Shukrani: The Knowing Of Her Spirit

Lucius Black

Independently published

Contents

Foreword

By all accounts, I should be some jaded version of myself, incapable of believing in love.

Within the expanse of thirty-five years, I have met my share of wonderful women and with them have told unique stories. A few of those have stuck with me and colored the hues of who I am today.

One story was of a first love, coupled with all the years and yearnings that two such intertwined hearts could make with and for each other. Although that story seems to have come to an end it makes me smile at intermittent times upon recollection.

Another tale was about the high school crush that became a situation all its own for two very different people. Here I'd be low to use the word 'relationship' given the tenuous nature of it all and my position as (á la my best friend's usually honest insistence) boyfriend #2. Playing second chair didn't suit me and it soured any feeling I may have had for her. That and a surprise engagement.

Of the stories, one of my favorites has always been the instance where two people met, vibed immediately, and fit in ways that touch beyond soul ties. In our differences we saw the beauty in each other while simultaneously catching sight of an equal. Yet time and again she was the one who almost got away for years and years. Much of that had been my fault.

Two of these sagas yielded the most learning for me as a man and a person.

The story of falling for a rare bird was a collection of starts and stops, rises and ruins, endings and beginnings. On the other side what could have been an exquisite soap opera were the realizations.

One had been that loving someone will not necessarily keep them. Because despite those goodbyes, there will always be some love for her in me. Things like that don't simply disappear.

After that, I also realized some ships were meant to meet and not to remain. That lesson stuck the most.

Upon meeting and loving a goddess in human form, I found a new brand of happiness. It felt good. I would even bandy about the word amazing. We seemed pointed towards great things. But what came to happen was that two people in two different places in their lives couldn't stay together. I had growing to do. For the most part I was thankful with the care in which she explained it all, teaching me that respect is part of loving someone and even leaving them.

There are other women with no less compelling additions to the timetable. I regret hurting them or not being enough for them.

Even with all this in my rear view, I still believe in love.

I'm excited about the idea of how fun it will be loving the right someone. And with that idea comes a question: what would I say to that woman?

This book says all those things and more in letters written to this future love of my life. I think this is something women need to hear and I am happy to share the words.

-LB

Introduction

Throughout this work you will see two words repeated over and over again. Both are words are Swahili words and are terms of endearment.

One is 'mpendwa'. It starts each piece and is referenced in the first letter. It means 'beloved'. The narrator addresses as beloved thirty-three times as proof of how beloved she is to him.

The other is 'mpenzi wake' (also referenced in the first letter). This one means 'her lover'. He calls himself this and tries to show her this in each letter. It's his identity and he thrives on being that for both her and himself.

Just a aside before you dig in.

Enjoy.

-LB

Cistern

Tuesday, May 16, 2023
9:48 am

Mpendwa,

(It's Swahili, love. Means 'beloved'. I wanted to start all these letters that way to let you know you are beloved in any language.)

The morning finds me somewhere between seasoning fresh flounder with a combination of Old Bay and lemon pepper and garnishing the whole grilled affair with parsley. Despite the tiredness that makes its way through me I intend to pour myself fully into preparing these dishes to the best of my ability. And it was that association that brought me to what it was I wanted to say.

For me, I don't lack confidence or trust in God's plan. Far from that. Most mornings are spent in an idling SUV thanking His name and seeking His guidance throughout the day. What plagues me has a foothold in all of us from time to time.

It's being disheartened.

I think we've all been disheartened or discouraged a time or two. The last time it happened the feeling stuck around, staying with me longer than I had expected. As an unwanted side effect, it colored what should have been certain, like the scope of a God-given talent. And it scared me how that could happen so easily by being saddened.

Then came you...

It's not some flying-in-with-a-cape superhero motion. It was just the strength of a woman showing itself as it always does in the most dire of times. And what I'd been feeling? Couldn't be more dire than that.

What you did was simple but powerful which, I've found, is the way you move often. There are other ways in which you move but we'll speak about that later.

When I see it in my head, I liken it to New Testament teachings about fine oils poured upon Jesus' feet. I'd never claim to be Him, but I understand what was being done then and now.

Whether I say it every time you do it or not, the act is so abundantly clear that I cannot help but see its glory. At the lowest you pour into me, freely giving me your faith and hope as if those same fine oils.

And that is heavy, something that weighs just as much as precious stones and gold.

To have someone believe in you so much that they pour their hopes, their soul deep beliefs into a sight unseen is amazing. Maybe that's why I push myself so hard as I do. Because you have given me that bit of you and all I want to do is prove how right you were to hold me in such regard. More than success or anything else, I want to show you that believing in me is the best bet you could have made.

More than that, though. I'm looking forward to the day when it's my turn. Ecstatic, really. Because there is a beauty in that reciprocity that I cannot say but will show when offered the opportunity.

I long to be the motivation when the world seeks to take yours.

I ache to be the loudest spectator in the stands, cheering just as your tired feet reach the final leg of the race.

I desire to be the support you need most when all else seems to turn to ruin and failure.

Simply said, I just want to be here for you. So, when I get the chance to pour into you like you've done me, I will fill you at your very emptiest.

Yours in love and life,
Mpenzi wake

(More Swahili. I'm sorry. Means 'her lover'. Because I do love you.)

You pour into me like living water. I pray I do the same for you.

Covet

Tuesday, May 23, 2023
11:45 pm

Mpendwa,

I couldn't sleep again. The late nights I set myself by taking this job keep me coming home long after the sun sets, and the flow of the world dies down. Nothing ever seems to be stirring when I finally get in.

Not even you.

And I can't fault you for that. If anyone works as hard or harder than me, it's you. I can almost see it in the posture your body has taken in bed. It's some wonderful punctuation to an otherwise boring set of sheets and pillows. Even the abandoned comforter by your feet knows you add something to the plain bedspread.

I'm digressing now and I'm sorry for it. Looking at you sometimes makes me do that.

And that's what I catch myself doing now, just looking at you. That simple act makes me understand a truth that I know to the soul, but I don't often say out loud enough.

Most of the day, even subconsciously, is spent missing you.

It's a chore to get up in the mornings and not because rising before the Sun is such a hassle. The difficulty comes when I must drag my body out of the vicinity of yours. Closeness feels akin to perfection, and I rob myself of it daily. But we need to be adults sometimes. So, I steel myself as I steal away from the marvels laced in your being, somehow not becoming anything like the metal in comparison.

Before I say it in the most eloquent ways I can, I say it in the most direct way. Forgive the lack of polish and the departure from the way with words I normally exhibit.

But...

Damn it, I miss you every day. Every damn day.

I miss the ever-present smirk that catches upon your lips when you look at me, sometimes becoming a full-blown grin and other times staying in its original form as you tease me.

I miss the scent on your skin. I'm convinced it's this commingling of citrus, flowers, and something else I can't quite place. At certain points in the day, I catch snatches of the fragrance. Without a bit of shame, I can tell you that I will look around for you for a minute or two. Not seeing you walking towards me proves to be a disappointment like no other.

I miss the way our eyes meet. Nothing in it is some smoldering romance novel type of exchange.

Romantic though I am, I like that it isn't.

What is it? It's simply looking into the eyes of someone I trust and believe in completely. What makes it better has to be seeing the reciprocity staring back up at me, clear and unwavering. Something as profound and uncomplicated as that feels like love more than getting lost in each other's eyes.

Because, truly, we often found each other there. And we continue to. Writing it makes me miss you all over again.

The poet in me wants to tell you every minuscule piece of you that I miss. But the pragmatist knowing what you'll say when you read these words says I should save the ink for another day. Over coffee and a rushed breakfast, you'll see these quickly scribbled encomiums.

Let's hope they make that smile come out to duel and rival the Sun itself.

Let's hope you're missing me as much as I'm missing you.

Yours in love and life,
Mpenzi wake

Our days are long, so full of things and moments. Just wanted you to know I miss you dearly and desperately.

Yin

Friday, June 2, 2023
2:56 am

Mpendwa,

The blessing and the curse of my mind is the ever-spinning nature it has about it. Maybe that's why I'm sitting up in the late watches scribbling out so many things. That usually happens when you let your gift reach a log jam.

Somewhere between a few easily written poems and a disagreement between myself and a fictional character of my own creation, I stop trying long enough to find myself on the Internet. As usual that sort of thing invariably moves to perusing social media.

The first thing that pops up is a picture of you.

It goes without saying that you're insanely beautiful as usual. But I say it because not speaking it feels like a wasted opportunity.

That running mind takes hold as I consider the digital photograph posted in the public domain. With each moment I take you in like one might readily consume the air. The conclusion or the set of deductions that follows catches me, making me think quietly before making me smile all over again.

The revelation?

There you be, this wondrous woman living light bright in her own autonomy and amazing purpose. You command the ground that you stand upon, even if the footsteps run towards the nervous sometimes. As if you didn't already know but you are power, life, and passion.

Everything and then more upon that. It's utterly awesome to see while simultaneously being frightening.

And that fear is mostly mine and has nothing to do with you directly. These frights come when I compare the vivacious soul to my more settled, earthbound temperament. To some it could exemplify steadiness and quiet resolve. Others might see it as being boring.

I think I can count myself as 'others' in the instance. Who am I to even stand next to you? What have done to be blessed to walk the same ground as this intelligent, infinitely unique individual?

Maybe nothing. But you chose me. We chose each other and that makes all the difference in the world.

Often in fairy tales, there is the innate need of another person as if we alone aren't complete unto ourselves. Looking at you I see the fullest version of a woman, of a grown person. At the most basic level, I'm not a necessity to your path. I respect that. But I'm what you wanted for that walk.

You wanted this sullen, quiet, introspective spirit to haunt the empty places we all have inside.

Much the same way I want the fiery, ambitious, calming heat to warm those cold rooms inside me.

Wants in this moment means more than the need. Having you want me as a component to your perfectly painted picture means more to me than you will ever know.

But then again...

...maybe you know now.

Yours in love and life,
Mpenzi wake

I understand that you are an individual unto yourself. You don't need me. But I'm thankful to be wanted by you.

Feast

Friday, June 2, 2023
11:07 am

Mpendwa,

It's almost lunchtime. The way my stomach is touching my back seems to signify this much better than the hands on the clock do. Inwardly I'm thankful for leftovers whenever we have the occasion to cook. This time we're partaking in what I cooked last night.

Creamy Tuscan pasta.

Despite your insistences and your worries about my well-being, I put shrimp in your part. Given that you don't have the allergies that I do, I wanted to do that for you. Because you enjoy them and are careful to brush thoroughly before you kiss me. It makes me smile how anxious you get and how cautious you are in that regard.

Last night went like it normally would when I cook. You're eager to help but I just want you to relax and let the smells of what I prepare wash over you. Like my personal ritual, I pour you a glass of your favorite wine and you sit on the counter.

Or rather I help you up. Something tickles me about beautiful short women and high counters.

Anyway...

Years of cooking have me doing my prep work as I hum to myself. Usually, you catch the beat of whatever I hum, and we end up singing in varying states of offkey hilarity.

The shrimp was cleaned (gloves on, of course), spinach chopped, garlic minced, and Parmesan grated.

Before too long the kitchen is a fragrant place and I can hear your anticipation like I'm hearing mine this close to noon.

Basil, garlic, sun-dried tomatoes, spinach. It all comes together with penne pasta and the ingredients to make magic. In about twenty minutes we are seated with pasta, a small salad, and garlic bread. We are quiet mostly save exchanged glances, contented moans, and laughter at sauce in my beard.

If I were being honest, I love feeding you.

But not just your empty stomach. In all the ways I can if you'll just let me.

Spiritually.

Now, I know I've been prone to a backslide or two in my lifetime. But it doesn't take away from how much I see Him in the things I do, how much I see Him in life here with you. Together I want us to pray in those better days and in those tougher ones when faith wavers. I won't waver because He never does. That example is what I can offer, when it is needed most.

Mentally.

I want to be the easing of your heavy burdened thoughts. Easy to say, I know. Still, you deserve relief from all the thoughts pressing down on you. They push without relenting and I just want to be the solace. Love, I can take the errant thoughts away if only for a little while.

And with that I would love to teach you while having you teach me. That exchange of life and lessons can only make us more than what we were the day before. Granted my wheelhouse is full of nerdy things about history and comic books, there are places where culinary tricks, deep analysis of literary works, and deeper things live as well.

Teaching even a fraction of that would make me happier than I could say. Learning from you would have a similar intoxication to it.

Emotionally.

It's fine to cry with me. It's perfectly fine to be mad too. I think it's the best measure of a love between two people when either can be vulnerable with their emotions. That's a safe harbor, a wonderful shore where you can be sure that what you feel will be heard and respected. Because it has seemed for a while that the evenflow between our genders has been a great lack of that. That can't be us. Trust me with your most intimate feelings and I will do the same with you. All the things we regard in low-spun places should never divide us.

Sexually.

Intimacy. Connection. In those moments you freely offer your perfect skin I want to move in a way that makes your breath catch in your chest, waiting for the eventual exhale. Also, I want to sate the primal parts of you and the parts that just want to be held into the night. All need my attention and I will give it each time it is desired.

For all the hunger that could affect my person, my woman...

...let me feed each one.

Amazing what leftovers can inspire.

Yours in love and life,
Mpenzi wake

One thing I want to do is feed you in all the ways you can be fed. Physically, spiritually, mentally, emotionally, sexually. However you may hunger, let me prepare that for you.

Recherché

Thursday, June 8, 2023
9:35 pm

Mpendwa,

Sometimes we speak of rarities and miracles in the scope of everyday life. I think if not for that beautiful phenomenon, life would be that much more mundane. Tonight lent itself to that credence and I smile while writing this.

It's a rarity for me to get home to you so soon, so quickly like I did today. As the sun quietly expired, I pulled up into the driveway. There was a contentment to it that cannot be measured accurately by mortal means. I'm sure you thought something similar when you heard my keys in the lock. Your whole body seemed to exhale as you caught sight of me putting down my laptop bag and walking toward you. As near as I can figure you were working on something. I've seen the posture enough to recognize it immediately, even when your entire course of your form switched at our reunion.

Clearly, you had already showered and were in a relaxed mode. I'm making inferences based on how comfortable you look as my oversized hoodie drowns you save for shapely legs and the infrequent view of your thighs.

That glimmer was enough to make a young man dream in those more intimate ways.

My eagerness may have outstripped yours in this moment as I take you into my arms. That felt like perfection, each second ensured in your arms and feeling your tempo all over again. Throughout the day I was offbeat but slowly, surely...I'm moving back in step.

An urge to pick you up, to grip your thighs strikes and passes in a moment. Within a second or two it returns when your excitement catches up to mine and passes it.

Eye to eye now. Your warm body and that intoxicating fragrance on you invades my nostrils as your Cupid bow lips mouth something that brings about a smile.

Missed you. That was all you said verbally since your physical was articulating much clearer and that much louder.

Each kiss reinforced it. Insisted upon it, in fact. I love how you do so much with something as wonderful as your kiss. Elsewhere I find myself between two heavens. One consisted of your lips upon mine. The other was my hands carrying your pleasing weight, a handful of warm thighs in each hand. Your skin has always been an addiction.

Today, though? More so.

When the intensity and the passion of the kisses distract me from carrying you to your highest height, your feet touch the floor again. I count five. Five steps backward as you survey me with this mixture of lust and intrigue. You start from my head and linger for the space of ten seconds on my beard. All I can do is smile. Blush a little too. That simple act encourages you, like always.

Further down. Further down still past scarred hands and arms, past waist.

A pause. Work slacks don't do much to conceal my desires for you and you stare. Openly and eagerly. Wordlessly you turn and walk away. I'm 99% certain where you're walking to but the way you cast off my hoodie confirms it.

I follow.

To be honest, I'm certain I jogged a little bit. I had to get to you.

Especially after you so seductively took off my hoodie and disappeared with that extra twist to your hips. Everything in me longed to be the reason and the remedy for that wrenching in your middle.

I come into the room to see you propped up in your elbows looking like a king's feast. Didn't really have a desire for dinner much but the idea and art of tasting you felt more appealing.

Clothes almost immediately became a liability and I got rid of them as you watched, patiently and at the same time hungrily.

I've always loved the idea of being wanted by you. In the same way, I have this innate thrill when I enter you. More than once I've likened it to coming home. We join again and match each other motion for motion.

I need to tell you what happened given your attendance and participation.

But what I can say is I'm thankful for the rarity of coming home early. Maybe I should keep it up if it always ends up with me intertwined with you. That's a want that goes so deep that no shovel could hope to find it, the sort of thing where a man longs after all that you are.

Or something like that.

Yours in love and life,
Mpenzi wake

There will never be a moment when all of me does not want all of you.

Lightning

Friday, June 9, 2023
12:35 am

Mpendwa,

It's strange to be lying here next to you sedentary, at peace and to be thinking about running.

Because when forced to think about it in something less than the abstract I did a whole hell of a lot of running. So fast and so far, I sometimes wonder how I even got back here to you.

Immediate things, immediate electricity bounding from one to another. That was the connection of two people who were introduced through a mutual friend. The thing was the commingling of intellect and growing twisted up in someone amazing.

I've always been twisted up in you, even in those times when I met wonderful souls and drew close. It took years to see it and more to admit it out loud.

Once you admitted that you feared getting caught up in me again. When you said it, I respected it more than I didn't like it.

Because that shit was true.

Truth is ugly sometimes, but it is ever-present in the spaces we make in our lives. I'd hurt you deeply and that was enough for you to desire to shake off those ties that once bound us. Thankfully I was smart enough to notice the change. Sadly enough, I didn't have the courage to chase you like I should have.

Strange how we kept finding ways back to each other on tentative footsteps. No one person wanted to step too close for fear of all that could or couldn't happen.

Skittish like a spooked stallion, we were. Still there was a communion between us. Love doesn't just die that easily. And we loved each other for years even if we never put the golden word to it.

Guess we were both ready to catch the ghost and race off then.

But we didn't.

There were a lot of conversations and hard admissions. They needed to happen a long time ago, but it was good that they came to fruition eventually. It was clear at the end of it all how much we still loved each other. That bone-deep sort of emotion that leaves an indelible mark on spirits. It made me know that mine had always been with you, even when we were both galloping off in different directions in our lives.

Nowadays the only running I do is chasing dreams, a brief thirty-minute jog before work...

...and running home to you.

That last one is my favorite. Especially if that takes me past a flower shop or something. Little gifts to make you smile in that way I've always loved.

Mostly I wrote this as an assurance that my running days are over. I've caught up to most of the things I really need, you being foremost among them.

Yours in love and life,
Mpenzi wake

I'm always going to come home to you. Nothing outside of what we're building matters as much.

Muse

Monday, June 12, 2023
11:35 am

Mpendwa,

From the moment you met me, you knew I courted the idea of dreams for my life and what I wanted to do with it. I remember spending a lot of time talking to you about it, telling you how happy it would make me to write for the rest of my days.

To your credit you did something very few people do when I open up and tell them the desires of my heart...

You listened and encouraged what I dreamt of becoming. That sort of faith means more than you could possibly know.

There is an infinite well of gratitude I wish to pour over you at every opportunity if I can. But this letter is about something more.

On the other end of those dreams coming true I court new ambitions and fantasies in the quiet times of the day.

One is you.

It's strange to daydream about you having just left our home, right? Tell me that it is. Because sometimes I feel like it might be. Then there are other moments where it feels like the most natural thing, almost like breathing or blinking your eyes might be.

I'm at work daydreaming about you in the simplest way. Today I'm fantasizing about past moments like the day we stood before God and bound ourselves one to the other. I tried not to cry but failed miserably. I have no shame about that because that day I met my future full force. If that isn't worthy of emotion, nothing is. As I watched you and your father walk in step with each other the realization really hit me.

This woman is it for me.

Maybe it was a long process of trials and errors because I had to see all the things that wouldn't or didn't fit. My best friend said something to that effect, and it changed my trajectory once she'd said it.

But once I knew, that was my truth. And that truly warms my heart and invades my thoughts. I remember looking down on you with this eagerness to do life with you and learn from you. It's still here but it was born that day.

I remember that whispered conversation your father...

...and dancing that first of many times...

...and just sitting at the head table hand in hand.

All the same, I probably should be working. But you sneak into the margins between poetry and prose, making me fall in love all over again.

Another dream from the eternal dreamer that came true.

Yours in love and life,
Mpenzi wake

You are it for me. I knew almost immediately.

Roots

Monday, June 12, 2023
1:39 pm

Mpendwa,

There all over again, back in that distant far-off land of make-believe and what could be one day. Facilitated by a full stomach and a quiet set of minutes without someone coming into my office asking me something, I daydream again. This time is a different flight of fancy, one steeped in the future and far beyond the past.

Kids.

Weird to be pondering kids now when the idea of being someone's father has scared me for so damn long. I think it may have been my single-parent household that made me wonder. An absentee father and a few piss-poor substitutes for the same made me think I was cursed. Cursed to repeat their mistakes and visit that ineffective run upon the next generation. I learned what lessons there were to glean from them, adding to what I got from my uncles and my grandfather in hopes of making a complete man.

And maybe it worked. Given the way I sometimes catch you looking at me in the peaceful hours, maybe I am whole after all.

Whole is good.

Even with that, I was always trepidatious about kids. I've played with and babysat my cousins' kids. Hell, I've watched my niece grow stronger all the time and been a part of that process.

But kids of my own?! Impossible. What if I mess it all up?

Loving you has given me courage that I couldn't have expected all while being extremely thankful for.

(The courage of love. Sounds like something I should write, right?)

With beautifully borrowed bravery bolstering my own I think of future generations a bit easier now. In fact, it's a wonderful thought that takes me away from deadlines and writer's block gripping me.

I dream technicolor dreams of little girls with your smile, your beauty, and your grace. Even though my first instinct would be to lock those daughters in the highest towers away from this cruel world, that would be unfair. Together I want to show them what love really is so that they never have to seek in all the wrong places or in the wrong arms. Maybe we can teach them strength and all they will need to navigate this cold world. Sound good?

I ponder sons in that same kaleidoscope of color. I'm hoping I can pass on my humility, my heart, and maybe some of my clever mind. And my weaknesses as well. Because I need them to be stronger than I ever was. Better men too. You were raised by a great man, and I value and treasure anything you can contribute to making our boys into great men one day.

Forward, maybe. But I long to lay these roots with you one day. Because we will be excellent at the task together. Like marriage, I'm sure rearing right them will come with its own challenges.

The woman I married, though...

...she laughs in the face of difficult things, much the same as the man you married does.

Yours in love and life,
Mpenzi wake

Of all things, I would love little ones who have your eyes or your

smile.

<h1 style="text-align:center">Renditions</h1>

Monday, June 12, 2023
4:20 pm

Mpendwa,

There are things said repeatedly, sometimes like a mantra or a prayer. Other times they are things said ad nauseum like an admonition or a reminder. For the sake of what I need to say next, I take the latter into consideration.

You know me well enough to know I have a quote that's apropos to what I need to say so here it is…

"It's the repetition of affirmations that leads to belief. And once that belief becomes a deep conviction, things begin to happen."

Muhammad Ali.

Champion thoughts. I'll borrow them briefly to elucidate this thought. And although I'm hyping it up beyond a normal measure, it's important to speak on.

I love you.

I'm certain this is common knowledge to you. Maybe you hear me faintly whisper it in the late evenings after a shower when I take my place in our bed. Sometimes I think you do judging by the way you move closer to me after the truest rumor escapes my lips. It's like your body punctuates mine like the perfect comma, so close and so wonderful.

It might be that you feel it in the lingering glances or the way my hands always find your body, whether it be to squeeze on you or just playful smack at parts to make you blush like you do to me.

It could be in the way I pray over you in those mornings before work. Most times you don't hear those heartfelt supplications, but they are all spoken with your good in mind. And mine as well since you are such an integral part of what makes my days so wonderful. Those five minutes I spent thanking Him for you while simultaneously worrying about you are interesting times to say the least.

Maybe it's the way my lips form your name. There is an inflection in it, a lilt in each syllable when I speak it. I've always hoped you noticed it, appreciated it even. And as observant as you show yourself to be I'm sure you've heard it. I would go so far as to say you might liken it to music. Because music hits the places we don't know we are vulnerable at. Here I am writing and hoping whenever I speak your given name or that sweet nom de guerre I made uniquely yours, that you hear a symphony of emotions.

With so many ways to show it, to intimate it...

...I'm hoping simply stating is beautiful enough too.

Yours in love and life,
Mpenzi wake

I love you. It sounds like a few simple syllables, but the emotions are so much more.

Mission

Wednesday, June 14, 2023
3:17 pm

Mpendwa,

At your best, you are love.

If The Isley Brothers and Aaliyah are to be believed as they belt out the timeless lyrics, your best is the truest showing of love.

But I think I disagree. It's done with no heat, but it's done because I've seen something to the contrary. I think I've seen the purest version of what we feel in your lowest times.

Let me explain.

Knowing you how I have and as long as I have has shown me many facets to the diamond that you are. There are days where you shine with a brightness and a clarity that puts the Sun itself on notice. I've been blessed to bask in those halcyon days with you. They were warm and wonderful. Even now as I remember them, I feel their warmth upon my skin.

As with any part of life there is a balance to it. Given that I've also seen you scraping the low places.

It was strange for me to see the brightest wings crumpled and wounded, falling here to Earth. One who didn't understand would call that sight a disillusionment of sorts.

But not me.

Why?

Because I have no illusions about who you are. I've seen that brilliant smile and I've seen it falter. I've seen you be less than the utter force of nature that I associate you with being.

And that's OK. Moreover, it's amazing. Imagine being so comfortable with someone that you allow yourself to come apart at the seams if only for a moment. In that moment I saw you clearly.

There was also a part of it where I learned who I was as both a man and as your partner.

As a man I have a capacity to be the rock upon which those hurting waves can crash, collide, and crest without breaking the resolve of the stone. Because there have been moments where tides of self-loathing or sadness threaten to pull you under. When that happened, you could reach for me, steady as I was, and ready to love you when you couldn't do it yourself. Finding that out about myself was a revelation to be sure, one of the better ones.

The part of me that is your partner found that I am equal to the challenge and ready to be what you need as you need it. You needed me to be your greatest fan when you were in the stands unsure, uncertain, maybe even feeling unworthy.

So, I was. Still am.

That's part of what I signed up for. To be your 80% when you have 20% left. Or to give 100% when you have nothing left. It's my job to be that.

What's different about this job is that I can't fail, won't quit, and I'm willing to work overtime at it.

Yours in love and life,
Mpenzi wake

Let me love you, even when you can't do it yourself.

Character

Wednesday, June 14, 2023
6:35 pm

Mpendwa,

I wanted to start this letter off by begging both your pardon and your forgiveness. Why I am asking for both will be apparent in a moment so bear with me.

Here goes...

People are drawn in by parts of a person and slowly fall in love with the whole as they discover more. Depending on when you ask me it's one of two things that drew me to you at first.

Some days I remember it being your smile. Those first conversations consisted of testing the waters and trading pictures between each other. I was flattered by how long you fawned over the hue of my skin, turning the word 'darkness' into something more than a word or a child's insult from long days past. Somewhere between basking in your praises, I took you in.

Your smile. It was a genuine thing, full of this playful wickedness and sweet summer sunshine all at once. I got to thinking it was the sort of thing everyone saw. Later and years on I found you only gave that grin to me and me alone. That made it more special, more like a gift you gave just to me.

Other days I remember it being your soul. Because in the beginning of us you and I exchanged way more than just pictures. We shared things that should never be wasted or given without conscious thought.

Our words.

With each dialogue, each quick poetic flourish, and each flirtatious aside…

…I felt a soul as big as the infinite space of a universe made more beautiful because you were in it.

It was and still is my evening star when it feels like the world clouds everything else, a warm light that tells me to come home.

Moments come where I think I know what you noticed about me.

I'm sure the skin tone is included in there given what I previously said.

Maybe my intelligence as well. It's one of my favorite things about myself so I would understand if it was one of yours.

My good heart maybe, a piece that is often at odds with my short temper for foolishness.

Whatever it was, I'm just glad to have been wonderful enough on that first glance and that you stayed to discover more of the man who pens this letter to you now.

But as you have found these stellar aspects to me, I'm sure there are the irksome pieces of me that can grate. Sometimes I'm just a sullen, quiet mess. Other times I try to be too kind to people who scarcely deserve it.

But what I speak of now is my ego.

Not ego in the sense of egotistical heights that would make even Kanye West blush. Nor do I mean it in that psychological way. I'm speaking of ego in the sense of self sort of way.

I've always moved with a strong sense of self and a decent enough idea as to who I am in the broad scheme. But sometimes it can get away from me. So much so that that ego won't let me do things, important things that could change the trajectory of the mission entirely.

One of those things is to ask for help.

I have you, strong and wonderful you. You're perceptive enough to see my struggle or damn near feel it coming off me in droves. You even asked...

"Are you OK? Is there something I can do?"

Could be it's a societal thing or just a bad habit I picked somewhere along the way. To me it's some paltry attempt to "save you" from whatever issue, struggle, or inner turmoil I've got going on.

And my ego would make me say, "No, love. I'm good."

But I gotta let that shit go. For myself and for you. We're in this together, right?

Being that we are I have to be stronger than I've ever been, strong enough to not be led by ego. My love wants to help me carry this heavy weight and I should be (and am) so thankful for that.

One time I called it a perfect heavy. It fits well here.

The heaviest part is that ego and I can let it go, just for you.

Yours in love and life,
Mpenzi wake

I'm a proud person. It comes with the territory of being a man. But no pride is as important as you. I can turn it down for you.

Piece

Saturday, June 17, 2023
8:35 am

Mpendwa,

I got to talking to an artist friend of mine the other day about painting. We went back and forth talking about watercolors and acrylics, perspective, light, and dark spaces. At the heart of the conversation was the theme of pictures and colors.

We as people are pictures of where we came from. By that same logic our parents colored us in so many ways, didn't they?

When I look at it, my mother is the main color of the masterpiece that I am. She passed on the deep reds of her passion for cooking, the steady grayscales of her work ethic, and the white-hot spots that do not suffer fools. I'm also thankful for my uncles playing that father figure role and lending me cool blues of soul, bright oranges of fire, and so many other tones.

The same is true of you.

Having met both your parents and spoken to them at length I can see what beautiful pigments they put into your life.

Strength from her, a certain steadfast golden color that comes off you like a wondrous living aura.

His kindness, catching deep brown flecks in your beautifully bright eyes.

While I looked at your colors so effortlessly, I saw something more that I wanted to touch on if you'll let me.

It's not every day or even every time I look at you. If anything, it's a passing flicker that makes me take a second glance at you. Most times I play it off as an extra appreciation of all the glamour your melanin presents. Other times I chock it up to zoning out for the briefest of moments. The way my mind often works lends credence to that and you rarely ask any follow-ups.

The truth is in those instances I catch sight of the duality of you. I'm thinking a lot of women have this happening.

I see the woman and the little girl.

And that sight lets me know what the work of my life must be.

Because the woman has seen the world through jaded eyes and is slow to trust and even slower to love. That verdant slash of color covered you before me and I've been giving my all in order to dim it. Seeing that little girl on the inside informs the second half of the mission.

When you were that little girl, I'm sure your father showed you everything a good man was by the way her treated both you and your mother. That bold and vivid purple carried into ideas of what her Prince Charming might look like.

Even now...

...despite the rough runs of the world, you want that for her. You need that for the girl you grew up with.

And me?

I want to be that. More to the fact, I need to be that. Being this ever-after avatar has the dual purpose of fulfilling your father's promises from childhood and his trust in my being the answer to that question he asked for his daughter.

The other part is helping the woman know down deep that the little girl is glowing bright yellow at being loved in only the best of ways.

A tall order and a masterpiece in the making. All the colors are there, and I will use all of them for the both of you.

Yours in love and life,
Mpenzi wake

Looking into your eyes I know I speak to both the woman who is and the little girl who was. As such, I will do my best to be gentle to both.

Ajar

Tuesday, June 20, 2023
7:15 am

Mpendwa,

I'm not a fan of the phrase 'unpopular opinion'. Because by their very nature, some opinions are innately unpopular. That's down to everyone being so different and so many different versions of a person. We see things through unique eyes and some thoughts can be misconstrued or interpreted in certain ways.

Owing to that dislike I just voiced, I won't preface this sentiment with that disclaimer. I think I'll just speak plainly.

A lot of people think locks are on doors to keep people out. I've never thought that, honestly. To me locks are there to protect what's on the inside.

Maybe that's a small distinction but one that needs to be made.

I felt (and sometimes still feel) your trepidation to let me in. It's not some large production but a subtle thing when asked a personal question or when a promise is made. When I see it, it's likened to a small twitch or a quiet retreat to safety.

A less secure man might see this and go into some diatribe about not being trusted or you hiding away. Although I have my moments of insecurity, none exist with this situation.

All I can ask is that you let me in.

Knowing you, I get that any padlocks and predispositions you have to being so guarded came from good reason and the need to protect the wonderful, wounded heart within. Self-preservation is a beautifully human response and shows more of the flawed beauty that I fell for.

Being human is to be just that - beautiful.

But let me earn the key to that gate, my darling.

And I will do that by showing you how I will honor and heal anything I find within. Those parts requiring worship will gain me as a willing acolyte of a new goddess. Conversely, those pieces in need of recuperation shall be tended to as if a doctor lived on call.

I'm aware that it isn't easy to let down the walls or to open that portico into your life. Nothing worth doing ever is.

Still, let me in. Acolyte or healer. Either or both. I'm here for it all. Here for you.

Just open up.

Yours in love and life,
Mpenzi wake

Let me in. I will honor what I see inside.

Unison

Tuesday, June 20, 2023
10:15 am

Mpendwa,

In three hours, I thought more about it, different words but a similar sentiment. I hope you won't be frustrated or annoyed by me doubling back if only for a moment.

In this coupling we have, I want to be the complement to everything that you are.

The savory that couples with the sweet.

The woodsy scent that precedes the tallest pine trees.

The predicate to you being the subject of everlasting adoration.

At its deepest we are two people trying to be safe havens in an existence where such solace leads to a near extinction.

Before I spoke about doors and walls coming down, being let into this fabled Shangri-La where you share everything and anything with me. The idea has its merits, but it should be something more, I think.

Becoming your happy place and your safe harbor means there will be no need for doors or opening them up. That trust, openly given, will eventually and irrevocably intertwine us in such a way…

…a way where there is no division between us two.

So now, having listened to my best friend for an hour or two, I have a better understanding of the nature of what I need to say, what I need to be.

I need to blend into you, a pair of wonders attempting to becoming one great wonderful.

And with that there is a greater intimacy as you are seeing into me and my dark corners as clearly as I can see yours.

Yours in love and life,
Mpenzi wake

Let me in. I will honor what I see inside.

Perpetuation

Sunday, June 25, 2023
6:45 pm

Mpendwa,

A civil war.

Most dictionaries define it as a war between parties, factions, or inhabitants of different regions within the same nation. They exist in living life and film. Hell, there are even a few in comic books.

I guess the same could be applied to a household as well.

Although...

I wouldn't say we were at war. At most it's a heavy disagreement and at least it's a small skirmish.

It can be said as a positive that neither of us yelled or called each other out of our names. That doesn't mean we didn't say things we maybe shouldn't have in our anger. Maybe that's why we went to our respective corners. Given all the quiet in a usually music-filled space, silence has taken on a deafening sound.

I'm inclined to call it a cold war more than anything. Each one of us is waiting for the other to make a move but there's a stubbornness in us that keeps us from it.

Eventually, we will. But things take time. God blessed me with patience so I can wait a little.

But not forever.

Even as write this, I imagine the beginnings of our tentative communications as they lead to the armistice before the reconciliation.

Although I'm low to admit it, I will falter once you look at me. Something about the way you look at me masters me in a way that I cannot rightly say.

And I'll look back, searching your eyes and your face.

Often on the other side of these discords, we do what we should have done in the first place, intelligent but emotional as we both are...

...and that was talk.

And sometimes that's the hardest thing to do. Because for some reason we want to hold on to the temporary feelings as if they are some permanent pressures. That's rarely ever the case with us. Often, we need the time to sort through the turmoil enough to begin the dialogue.

We'll go back and forth, wading into the depths until we come out to the other side.

Then it ends...

...sometimes with playful chiding...

...other times it's a lingering embrace...

...or kisses given...

...or even the bearing of souls and skins.

However, we end it, I will always be thankful for our permanence winning out over a temporary bump in the road.

Yours in love and life,
Mpenzi wake

Sometimes, we'll be angry. But temporary motion is not a permanent situation. With time and talk, we will come through it.

Ballad

Friday, June 30, 2023
10:28 am

Mpendwa,

The way a person's mind associates with certain things has always been something I am deeply interested in. One of the things that garner strong associations has always been music. Certain songs play and they transport me to various moments or make me feel certain emotions behind them.

For as long as I live "Dear Mama" will make me think of the hard lessons, the laughter, and the person that my mother is. The two are all but inseparable.

That Adele song "Hello" reminds me of a gut-wrenching feeling and myself acting so out of character that it sometimes amazes me still. That melody catches hold and remember the wasted tears for someone who may have never deserved houseroom in my heart.

As you well know "Slow Motion" is my number-one song. It takes me back to middle school and the first time I heard it. It also transports me to a few parties and some slow grinding moments.

I named those few to give examples and segue into what I really want to say but you know there are plenty more. You've heard me more than once singing them around the house.

We've had discussions, you and I, about "being seen" and if the other provides that. According to you, that's something I do so easily. I'm always glad to do it for you too.

Your uncertainty shows during these talks, where nervous lips ask if you do the same. Invariably and unequivocally the answer is yes.

But when I think of seeing you clearly and loving you for everything that you are a song comes to mind. To me, it speaks to an enduring affection between two people and how connected two souls can really be.

The song?

"No One In The World" as sung by Anita Baker.

I hear it in playlists on my phone or in the car frequently and I sing it every time. More and more as I listen to the words, I can see the roots of our story in it. The verses speak to people away from each other who are never truly apart from each other.

And the hook is what I feel when we look at each other, touch, inhabit the same spaces, or just quietly exist together.

Over and over it plays in my head like a reminder of something I know I could never forget. The talented contralto always shows me the same thing as her voice is set free by those wonderful lyrics. And what she shows me has command of both my eyes and my loudly beating heart.

I see you, love. Clearer than anyone else might or ever has. And there is no one else in the world like you.

Yours in love and life,
Mpenzi wake

Can I see you? Of course. I see you more clearly than anything or anyone else that I look at.

Marvel

Sunday, July 2, 2023
11:15 am

Mpendwa,

So many things can be counted as miracles here within our walks of life. The first one I think of is the miracle of childbirth.

Someday I pray for that blessing in our lives because I know our nature and how wonderful we would be in those roles, how we would together as parents.

Next, I ponder rainbows, the stars in the night sky, and beautiful occurrences that cannot be put into words.

You know the type, right?

Happenings that mostly make you feel and know there to be a presence of God or something greater than us.

As always when I think blessings like that, you appear in my mind's eye.

Because I know you as well as I do, I'm sure you read that last sentence as skeptically as possible. That was probably then followed by a small pout/smirk combination at me calling you out so easily.

Before you dismiss it, let me tell you more.

It takes a lot to walk on water unless you're Jesus. As for us mortal folks, it takes depths to wade through the waters of life.

Sometimes the tides push against us, threatening to carry us away into the deep waters where too many have been lost. Other times we question our place amid the waters, doubting our strength to move the seas with enough force.

Most mornings I watch you since you tend to rise before I do. Immediately I find hypnotic beats in your sway and your gait. Sometime after I hear the shower and you singing along to your morning playlist. As I get up you are brushing your teeth or doing your hair. I've caught you taking six steadying breaths in the mirror a time or two.

Always six, every time like clockwork.

Immediately after you smile faintly. I can't tell if it's a grudging smile or a resolute one. Whichever it you, you kiss me softly in passing and go to your closet.

That is you marshaling your powers, powers in the sense of a strength that keeps you during the days. I feel like I'm watching magic happen when you do this.

Your magic.

And I'm proud.

Because this is the miracle of you. It feels simple but it isn't.

You're a beautiful, brilliant Black woman who takes on the world every day without losing yourself to it. While I will never fully know the mechanics and motions of living in your skin, I am in awe how easily you seem to navigate it. And while that may be something of a masquerade, you never let it slip until we reconvene at home.

And as you talk, as you lay it all out over a glass of wine and me making your favorite…

… I am seeing my miracle live in living color.

Maybe I don't truly know the definition or scope of it all the time, but you perform a miracle daily with getting up and being the best version of yourself.

One of those things that makes me want to love you and love on you just a little more.

Yours in love and life,
Mpenzi wake

Every day you make me proud. Not by doing some Herculean task. Mostly by just getting up on the bad days and doing miracles with it. I'm in awe.

Nonpareil

Monday, July 3, 2023
12:17 pm

Mpendwa,

There isn't some deep introduction here or some clever segue into what I want to say. Not this time. As such, I'm just going to start writing.

You are my treasure.

Every part of your existence shines like the brightest gold and warms the places in me that feel made of shadows or a perpetual cold. That makes you special in and of yourself.

But there's more, so much more.

I treasure your energy. Sometimes I liken it to that sheer elation a kid feels catching fireflies on summer nights. Your presence makes that same euphoria thunder against my ribcage as my heart beats quicker.

Quicker yet somehow steadier.

Even with not a word exchanged having you there feels like a long embrace on a windswept autumn night. And here I am craving it in the middle of summer.

Each part of yourself shared is a gift. Whether it be the way you hum softly as you clean or how certain songs make you sit up and pay attention. Experiencing this or just watching you live in the parts of the whole is amazing. It's almost like watching a cinema in a panoramic view.

I could go on and on here. And I would if that's something you'd be interested in reading, but I think I'll end on a simple note.

Piracy of the high seas amounted to the theft of goods and treasure as many legends will have you to believe.

Gold, diamonds, precious stones. All sorts of valuables.

Imagine now how jealous all those peg legged Petes, and high seas raiders would be now to know that I am in possession of such a treasure.

Brighter than gold.

More flawless than any diamond.

More precious than any earth dug stone.

That's you. Always and ever after.

Yours in love and life,
Mpenzi wake

Treasure. You are a treasure bound in beautiful flesh. Sometimes I remember that and smile all over again.

Mezzo

Wednesday, July 5, 2023
3:45 pm

Mpendwa,

Two people, insomuch as they share basic similarities, are as different to each other as opposites could be. All this happens while being comparable in placements and stature.

Equal opposites, actually.

I'd been thinking as much for a long time. Admittedly, it bothered me slightly towards the beginning of everything we would become.

Because looking at myself I saw this simplistic man, with no frills about himself playing that role to perfection. It didn't reach my notice until the blessing of you.

Eyes wide open and with deep inhalations, I took you in. Detail by detail, moment after moment. In learning you that way I saw the crux of who you were.

Enter this classy, divine woman with a gracious smile and these gorgeous eyes looking back at me. I hadn't been sure of hearts being able to skip multiple beats until that moment. It was reinforced with each second that followed where you kept to my orbit...

...even if, honestly, I thought sometimes I didn't deserve the gravity of the two-planet mambo we found ourselves in. Or I didn't deserve that special way your eyes framed me at times. That stare lived somewhere

between adoration and awe; an addiction once first seen that could never be shaken.

I was hooked.

Far past my nervousness or my need to be clever around you...

...or that ache to just hold you and never let go...

...you became my addiction. Not pharmaceutical in nature but a wonderful habit of its own name.

It feels cliche to say, 'opposites attract'. If I were to modernize it or give it a more up-to-date credence, I'd say the opposite fit the bends and bows of each other.

Loving you is easier than breathing more days than I can count. Even without being so dissimilar in so many ways, we find routes and roads towards making this thing of ours work.

I'm guessing that's a team effort.

Because we work at it with soft kisses and softer words as needed. Your tenacity for us being the best versions of ourselves plays into it. So does my optimistic nature and the dreamer's heart I carry. Somewhere in the median of so many things, they collide and make our peace.

Glad to be a piece of that and of you.

Yours in love and life,
Mpenzi wake

Two people with two sets of ways. Somehow, we fell in love. And somehow, we'll find the middle ground between the two routes.

Pax

Friday, July 7, 2023
6:45 pm

Mpendwa,

Si via pacem parabellum.

It's Latin.

Since you know me as well as you do, you probably guessed I stole the words from either a movie or a book. In this case, a movie. The meaning caught me and didn't let go given the simple elegance and truth behind it.

"If you want peace, prepare for war."

I think it's safe to say we all desire a certain level of peace in our lives. Music and writing equate to my peace as much as anything might.

Often you do too. You are part of the deep thrumming harmony in my world. It's both an honest statement and a very sweet one.

But just as honestly, I can say that sometimes you are not.

There are times where we disagree, or we take upon heated words as if no other syllables will do the job. Those days were storms, love. No question about it. I remember one night our collected fury led to my downstairs trotting to the couch armed with a pillow and a blanket.

Upset was the immediate feeling. But I learned a long while ago that sometimes our first feelings are wrong.

Mine were when measured against everything.

Because we yelled instead of talking that night, I cannot speculate on what you might have been feeling. All I can say is what I felt in all the minutes after we exploded.

Mostly, it was loneliness. I've grown so accustomed to sharing a space and a bed with you that my absence made me ache for you.

I don't ever want to do that again. Not one more night.

The disagreements? That's going to happen a time or two. As much as I celebrate how different we are from each other, I recognize that means we see things differently as well. That friction can start the fire and could burn us down if we let it.

My suggestion?

Going forward, we remember that this momentary discord is our chance to come together and suss out the problem. Attacking each other yields bad feelings and neither of us deserve that.

You deserve my compassion, my patience, my understanding. Just the same I need yours if we are to work through those moments.

Point of fact, I need you more than I would ever need to be right.

You're my peace of mind and our almost-wars should end with peace in your mind and mine.

Yours in love and life,
Mpenzi wake

Together we can take on the problem, not each other.

Healer

Monday, July 10, 2023
6:30 pm

Mpendwa,

Sometimes, there is a danger in knowing. Because knowledge can be a curse in certain situations. Some truths have a weight to them that can hurt.

We've all been told a secret honesty about someone we saw in one way. It altered that perception and simply knowing what you did felt like a deep cut.

Conversely, knowing some things can be a joy or a privilege.

Like knowing a favorite song or person.

You know me.

Deeply, intimately, almost down to the bones. And I know you that way as well. It's a source of jokes and feigned annoyance between us. One of those sweeter aspects of this love we have.

When I came into the house as quietly as I did, you noticed. There wasn't a lack of affection between us because you are always the high point of my days.

But something was bothering me, even if I didn't say anything about it.

To your credit, you didn't press. Despite the promise to be open with each other, to share our worlds with each other you know this foolish nobility I have about me. I don't ever want to bury you with the worries of my day...

...which reminds me of an old friend's insistence on doing a disservice by not sharing the pains along with the pleasures with someone you care about.

You enter the room. I start talking. Maybe for about twenty or thirty minutes which, given my often-terse nature, is an amazing thing. Quiet meets my conclusion as I look at you.

You look back.

Then you do something so uncomplicated yet so powerful. You embrace me. Granted the height difference is ever-present but negligible as I lean low enough for your arms to ensnare my neck.

And I breathed slowly, probably for the first time that day. I know the cause must be your hands on me.

Your hands heal, whether you ever knew it or not. I've seen it many times in practice, and this is another instance.

When you take my face in your hands, your fingertips produce warmth, electricity, and this magic that has no name but I'm always thankful for.

Softly you ask me to look at me. Without hesitation I do it, falling in love with your eyes all over again as the static in your palms quickens my heartbeat.

"I love you, I'm proud of you, and you matter...always."

This is followed by my quiet tears as you kiss my face all over and keep your hands on my face.

Between embraces, soft kisses, and affirmations I come back to myself. Like the ebb and flow of us, I cook all your favorites in hopes that the love I put into everything speaks my gratitude my lips tried to voice an hour ago.

Doctor lady of mine, healing me with these hands of yours. I'm thankful for them every day.

Yours in love and life,
Mpenzi wake

Your hands are healing. Much the same as your hips and hopes. Place them all upon me as often as possible.

Faults

Wednesday, July 12, 2023
7:59 pm

Mpendwa,

As we want to do some nights, we unwind after equally long days with snacks, libations, and jazz music throughout the house. What starts as slow dancing, singing too loudly and hearty laughter becomes an exercise in sedentary life before too long.

The plush couch plays the backdrop as we intertwine. Amid that, we talked a little quieter than we sang and sipped something potent.

This particular day was an aged scotch you'd bought and thought we might enjoy when the occasion called for it.

It came and it was called for.

What I liked most about the conversation was how unassuming it was. Innocuous things like lunch or what kind of perfume you wore today.

Whatever it was I liked it.

There is a closeness with certain people where words are unnecessary because you just understand. I've had that with friends and family both. It surprised me how easily we got to that after we'd first met. Even into the current, it persists like lingering smoke, and I pray it never dissipates.

Quietly lost in each other I caress skin wherever my fingers find it. Mostly I hear small, ticklish laughs or a contented sigh in response.

But one spot it two elicits a shift of clothing and the briefest trace of a smile.

One of your least favorite parts, a flaw by your definition of it.

I can't scoff at it or disregard it because we all have those inward critiques of ourselves that only we see. I've always been that way about my feet. It's why I keep socks handy.

Somehow you like my big clown feet, so much so that you've stood carefully on them to kiss me a time or two. Even when you make fun whenever I buy sneakers, I feel the acceptance and love coming off you in waves.

That patch of skin or whatever flaw you think you see, I love you for and in spite of your insistence to its existence. Moreover, even with that you would always be my choice each time the option was given.

Maybe that's too many words so I say this instead, a whisper colliding perfectly with Boney James and Dave Koz.

"You know I don't care about that, right? God lent me perfection so stop hiding it..."

Any falters to that grin die off when I say this. Skin to skin again we just allow the night to happen around us, flaws and all...

...even with us knowing those tiny imperfections play as nothing measured against the home we've built. This is just a reminder for when you need to remember.

Yours in love and life,
Mpenzi wake

Flaws and all, I will keep choosing you like you keep choosing me.

Lesser

Friday, July 14, 2023
9:15 pm

Mpendwa,

There seems to be a divide growing between men and women, this place where our beliefs in each other fade within the passing of the days.

For the part of women, they feel unprotected and unseen in the world.

Granted a man could see her in the sense of physical attractiveness or a desire to touch her in all the most intimate ways. But not in the ways that matter the most.

Maybe that is why most women hear a man talking and almost immediately believe him to be a liar and his words nothing but folly.

To the counterpoint of the men, we all feel the need and desire to wanted for the person more than the material aspects.

Now I understand security is a large part of what a woman seeks in her partner. I respect it. But many men have been used for what they have by less-than-stellar beauties and the aftermath is a certain trepidation.

I guess what I'm getting at is this...

No one wants to be reduced to less than what they are.

Maybe that's why I listen to you so intently when you speak. I tend to hang on to the words like leaves in the highest trees. I will admit to finding myself disagreeing with certain points of view and having a different way of seeing the same.

And when I say this, I never want you to fear anything in the statement.

Because I would never say the way you see this world, or the issues therein are crazy or wrong. That is a reduction of your brilliance and the sight of both your eyes and your soul. Those are two things I would never want to bring low.

My every desire is to take you to those high places you deserve.

Even if I can't see the vision or understand as fully as you would like me to, I will always respect both.

Call it part of loving you like I do.

Yours in love and life,
Mpenzi wake

Calling you 'crazy' feels reductive, unworthy of you. I will do my best to listen to a perspective that isn't my own. Even if I don't always agree.

Audience

Saturday, July 15, 2023
12:44 pm

Mpendwa,

I think it started in childhood, my interest in putting things together and building all sorts of diverse items. I'm sure it would come as no surprise to you that I was one of those kids with Legos and Erector sets. My imagination knew no bounds and everything I built seemed to reflect that.

All of that informed a meticulous nature and this draw towards things that need to be fixed or assembled.

Ceiling fans.

Outdoor sheds.

Bookshelves.

Under the tutelage and the exasperated sighs of my mother, I became good with my hands. I literally own a book full of do-it-yourself projects that I can't wait to delve through deeper.

I'm a fixer.

A lesson I've been learning with you has been that not everything requires what you've deemed my "handyman energy".

There are times when you talk at length about moments that seem to aggravate the very soul in your body. My mind starts working fast for a panacea or some answer to the problem.

That damn "handyman energy" at work again.

It's hard sometimes to turn off my brain and just listen. Something has helped with it, though. I'm reminded of a certain moment when I can.

Audio midnights.

What started as something of a plot device in my stories became a term I used in conversation, one that even rubbed off on you amazingly enough.

It's that area of time where lovers lie still in the quiet of the night, satisfied and just listening to the cadence of each other's hearts.

And that's what I'm doing now, only in a different way. You're lending your heart with your words as opposed to the after-effects of what our bodies do so perfectly together.

Either way, I just want to lie here and listen.

Yours in love and life,
Mpenzi wake

My nature is to fix things, offer solutions to problems. But you need to vent occasionally. So, I'll just listen.

<h1 style="text-align:center">Requite</h1>

Tuesday, July 18, 2023
7:30 am

Mpendwa,

It would take more than fingers or toes to enumerate the instances where I took advantage of the innate strength God lent to your skin and your spirit. Despite being a man, it feels disingenuous to act as though never draw power from you. And I don't want to be made a liar to save face. That resilience came from places that I've already touched on in previous letters. But they bear repeating.

Your healing hands.

The way your eyes frame me as if I'm some sort of superhero despite my being as flawed as the next man. Maybe even more sometimes.

That big and beautiful soul that shines out into the infinite spaces of the world.

Those examples and all the other merits in your arsenal have revived and fortified me on days when I felt the world was doing its best to shatter spirits and break bonds of good hope.

If I never say it enough, thank you. From the depths of me.

Or maybe I can show that appreciation.

Because this morning as we let light shine into the windows, dawn was punctuated by the soft sounds of your tears. For a while I didn't move, merely listening. When the waters persisted, I asked what was going on.

"I just don't feel strong enough today…"

I understood. It was easy to because of how many times I've felt the same without being too intimate it so succinctly and so clearly. The realization hit me that you needed me almost immediately. Today I woke up feeling as though I could conquer all that stood before me.

But the love of my life didn't.

So, I set out to give you what you have given me innumerable times before.

Just a little bit of my sound footing.

So, I pulled you closer, curving my body against yours like a shield. Then I kissed your cheek softly, using my right hand to wipe away an errant tear.

Then I spoke.

What I said wasn't profound or overly eloquent like you've come to be used to from me. There were even a lot of words used. But I think they may have been the right ones.

"I want you to stay here with me. Take whatever strength I have until you can stand, OK?"

Seeing your nod gave me the briefest of smiles as we lay there, you marshaling your powers and me just happy that I could begin to return all the favors of the same color you'd done for me.

Yours in love and life,
Mpenzi wake

Take some of my strength when it feels as if you aren't strong enough. You've done it so many times for me, so I want to return the favor.

Edify

Friday, July 21, 2023
10:45 pm

Mpendwa,

I can admit openly and excitedly to how much of a craving every inch of your skin exercises over me. Thinking now of the quality collection of curves, falls, dips, and soft places takes hold of my mind as I write this now.

And thought seems to be the issue, doesn't it? Although issue may be the wrong word if I was to be honest with you.

Allure might be better.

At my core, I've always been attracted to the mind of a woman. Somehow, I've courted women who carried both beauty and brilliance in spades a time or two.

You surpass them all. And by doing that you have reached that essence of who I am and piqued its interest in past words.

Or maybe just the one.

Sapiosexual.

A person who finds intelligence to be a sexually attractive quality in others.

Me to the letter.

Because I could listen to you tell me about anything that falls under your expertise. Part of me thinks it's the confidence with which you elucidate these facts and figures...

...making me that much keener to explore your figure knowing the powerhouse of a mind leading the whole package.

There is such an arousal in the dialogue where we discuss any manner of subject. As with any conversation, there should be this exchange of thoughts and ideas. Admittedly, my heart goes quicker in the tempo when I learn something or a point you've made catches me.

(I had a clumsy double entendre about deep talks and deeper things after, but it feels unnecessary now. Instead...)

The expanses of your mind lead me into wicked thoughts of exploring the spectra of your body, slowly and with earnest hands. I say earnest because this had been a quid pro quo sort of situation. You had been so keen to teach me, and I would, in return, be ecstatic to be your instructor if for these stolen moments.

In those moments I show you the effects of a beautiful mind on a man who has become a student of wanting you, needing you in the closest ways and avenues of intimacy.

With a mind being a terrible thing to waste, I intend to waste not one word, one thought, or one action.

Yours in love and life,
Mpenzi wake

Your mind is as beautiful, as sexy as every inch of your body.

Dyad

Saturday, July 22, 2023
9:30 am

Mpendwa,

The smartest thing anyone can do is to never expect perfection. When I met you all those summers ago, when I fell in love almost in that instant there was never any anticipation of a flawless person.

Maybe that was why I saw you so clearly in an instant.

It was those small things, the idiosyncrasies, and the tiniest traits, that made you more beautiful to me the longer we talked. And we talked for such a large space of time. Hours didn't seem to matter outside of their passing and a faint cognizance of it.

Even now I remember that time and I smile.

Here into the present painted by the past, I recognize how different we often are while understanding how incredible that fact is. Opposites attract, often finding a certain equity in each other if the fit is right enough. And we have always had that even when distance and other hands took hold of us.

On the other side of so many stories we told with our open hearts and eager footsteps, we found each other again.

This time, I'm not keen on releasing your hand or squandering this chance again.

Because I have seen the newest versions of those same people, and they are magnificent together. Still as different as before but with a fresh set of eyes on life. Somewhere along the way we became of one mind, wanting similar things in the intersections while each still seeking out our personal goals.

And I want to do that work with you by my side. Helping you achieve every desire of your heart while building a beautiful commingling of an ever-after seems to be what I was built for.

There is no need to ask of your particular brand of reciprocity since I have seen how you poured into me long before this union took center stage. I don't question you as my equal and opposite.

Not now or ever.

I'm thankful every day for your lack of conventional "perfection" while realizing our different manners and your comparable heart make you perfect for me.

Yours in love and life,
Mpenzi wake

Although we are of two different minds, we are of the same heart.

Days

Monday, July 24, 2023
1:28 pm

Mpendwa,

Blessings have come into our lives in multiples that we often don't think too much of. We have been gifted two eyes to see the beauty of God's works and five senses to experience the bounty those works could offer.

Each sense by itself is a godsend of its own, one worthy of all sorts of lyrical asides that I won't get into just now.

What I've been thinking about of late is something we have been given just one of.

(That mostly depends on who you ask, though.)

That solitary allotted gift is a lifetime.

Many people have a fairly good idea what they will send theirs doing. There are pursuits we all seek to complete with our singular walk amongst the roses and thorns. Whatever people choose, it touches many gamuts of their lives.

Emotional, spiritual, professional, physical, social, biological, etc.

For me, my dream for so long is to write for the rest of my life. I would know the truest happiness if I could tell the world my stories for all the time I have left.

Another thing I want to do is raise a family. Despite my trepidations at times, I know there is so much I could be for a wife and some children. It's too much to list but I have the strength and the heart for it.

The list also consists of seeing God one day. Flawed though I am, to be in His presence would make everything worthwhile.

Lastly, I want to spend part of this lifetime learning everything I can about you and how best to love you.

You surprise me in all the best ways, whether it be by quoting one of my favorite songs on the fly or having some profound insight that I could have never seen.

I'm floored sometimes by the methods to which you show me, weird nerdy me, how much it is you love me. Once it was a random gift, something that most men aren't conditioned to receive. There was even a note with a succinct little explanation behind its purchase. Even now I smile at it from its place on the desk in my office.

Your words show it too. There are little appellations we sometimes honor loved ones with. Each one you've given me feels like a faint little kiss upon my very soul.

Most of what you say encourages, believes, and teaches me. And I need all those things in ways you may or may not know.

It's only right that I strive with this life to make you feel as much or more of that electric thrill you strike me with daily.

You deserve that and I hope a lifetime is enough to learn the roads and take you to those hallowed places of my whole appreciation.

Yours in love and life,
Mpenzi wake

Learning you will take a lifetime. Allow me all the time I need.

Muddle

Tuesday, July 25, 2023
5:37 pm

Mpendwa,

I rode home in my truck thinking about us again. It wasn't some deep, loving thought at first. If anything it was a profound one that became more as the processes went on.

Allow me the opportunity to share.

When I look at us, we are, essentially, a mess as people. And I think that may be the same for most of the world. We are all constantly dented, dinged, done dirty by the rough edges of a hard world. But slowly I figured out the secret of it all in your embrace and in your esteem.

What to know what it is?

It's the simple fact of understanding that part of living. We all must see our own chaos and figure out how to work through it. This is made easier when you meet someone battling with their own mishmash internally. Because sometimes, if we're lucky, that person we meet is sometimes willing to help us sort through the muck.

By God's grace, I ended up loving you. I've always extolled that power and heard it spoken of in verse and song. But nowadays I see it in the most practical and elegant of ways.

At my core, I'm a whole lot of messed up. I'm man enough and honest enough to know that. Maybe it's the heartbreak or any number of things that made me feel like some cluttered human seeking some small moment of light. However you say it, that's all I think I've ever been seeking.

Then came you...

To be clear I never expected you to save me. That was never your job. What you did was somehow better than that.

You came with your mess, meeting mine as I met yours. Not once did you flinch and neither did I. Together, we took the time to sort through our shit while loving each other in the best ways.

By listening.

By supporting.

By being there for each other.

Somewhere between all that we started reaching hands into each other's problems, offering kindness and calm amid the tumult. There were times when I couldn't tell you which felt better: being the shore to which your high tides could break or you showing me the way in a room that I always thought had no doors.

Things come together and we figure out the way through. I could have done the work without you. Just the same you could have navigated it all successfully like you always do.

Still...

It is a gift to have you at my back as we clear up the mess. Together at that.

Yours in love and life,
Mpenzi wake

You're a mess sometimes. So am I. Maybe we should work on that. Together.

Simply

Thursday, July 27, 2023
7:50 pm

Mpendwa,

Despite what I need to say here, I'm going to try to be brief. Which may be hard given the weight of what I want to say to you.

Here goes.

Love of my life, I am a lot.

Admittedly, I portray myself as a simple man. In more instances than one I am. But emotionally, mentally…

A lot.

And it's never your intent or your wish to saddle the people you love the most with that burden. But sometimes it is unavoidable when it's a part of who you are. So, I embrace it tentatively, trying to master this piece of the entire man.

Now I know we spoke of being a mess and being each other's mess. You're my favorite mishmash and I love you despite of it and because of it. Yet on my end of the heap, I worry. I worry that I'm making your part too difficult, too heavy to bear outright. Chalk that up to my mind working overtime while trying to preserve you and your sanity.

Maybe that's the point.

Trying.

I see it in how you'll sometimes find quiet when I probe too deeply into a problem. Most times I let it go or allow you that benefit of the doubt. It took this long to realize that you were protecting me in your own way. It's brave and wonderful of you.

Knowing this now, I want to be more of those things.

I'll always let you in. But I will do my best to make the process easier for you. Because I've never been as easy as a Sunday morning.

But maybe, I can be easy enough for you.

Yours in love and life,
Mpenzi wake

It won't always be easy, but I will try my damnedest not to make it too hard.

Resign

Friday, July 28, 2023
6:25 pm

Mpendwa,

The reciprocity between us is one of those unspoken parts of this love affair of ours that warms me. To have someone show me what I show them in an equal measure is a beautiful daydream of mine come true.

One of the things we reciprocate is an innate inability to give up on each other. I can't say where yours found its origins.

But I know where mine was born.

I was the firstborn, my mother's only son. Chalk it up to being the child of a single mother. While she did all the hard work to make sure we had a roof over our heads, things for school, and food in our bellies she made sure to teach me. I took on the responsibility quickly and almost effortlessly.

Between her, neighbors, uncles, and a praying grandfather I learned a litany of things like using tools, building things, basic electrical work, and basic car maintenance. Little did I know they were all teaching me a greater lesson.

Tenacity.

I can remember putting up ceiling fans with novice hands and small drawn diagrams, my mother's voice in the background. Sometimes I didn't get it on the first try. When I didn't, I kept going. There was no backup in me as I kept fiddling until I found the right way.

That translates into so many parts of my life now that it feels as if it had always been there.

This is where you come in.

That tenacity translates into my steadfast support of those who I love and trust. Even in my maddest moments, I don't surrender to letting go of my loved ones. I may step back or leave them to their devices, but they are never far from my heart.

You are a special case.

You have never been too far from my heart. If I were honest, maybe it was always with you when we were apart. Too many times life has divided the road between us. But I have never given up on you or in wishing you well with all my energy. Now, on the other side of finding each other, it's easy to continue that pattern.

Not because you have done it in all the most wondrous of ways.

But because you are a bone-deep part of me as a person and that kind of caring lends itself to never giving up.

Yours in love and life,
Mpenzi wake

You don't make a habit of giving up on me. Much the same, I won't do that either.

Fathoms

Saturday, July 29, 2023
11:25 am

Mpendwa,

One of the easiest things in the world to do and, simultaneously, the most engrossing thing I could do is look at you. It tends to be an obsession too often. To your credit, you seem not to be bothered by such devotion. If anything, it makes you smile wide and wonderfully in the atmosphere. That moves to the cycle where I want to look at you just that much more.

But what am I thinking as I do?

Several things if you're curious to know them all.

Sometimes I see you lying on the couch reading some book with your music playing softly in the background.

My immediate thinking leans towards curiosity as to what the book was about.

My next mind focuses on beauty. Because you are a feast for the eyes, one that is liable to make sight satisfied.

Then I'd lose myself to your curves again, lingering on the question of how you'd respond if my lips found the dip between hips and ribs. Ticklish or turned on are the answers, even if I'm never sure which it will be in the immediate nature of the moment.

Proud is always a thought looking at you. Because you make feel it as

I watch you grow and progress. I'm always impressed at how you took and till, planning for the next season of your life with such an aplomb that I often wish to borrow even a tenth of it.

Lucky too. God blessed me with you, and I can also speak to the luck of two divergent paths converging in the ways ours did.

But you know my most prevalent thought tends to be?

I ponder the depths of you as both a woman and a person. Or rather as my woman and my person. When I think of that I know there are deeps where I have yet to reach or see clearly.

And that intrigues me to no end.

The hope of a life with someone is to know them and their depths in an intimate and profound sort of way. Despite the love thundering in my chest and seeping through my pores, I know there is more of your worth loving and knowing. I want to spend days diving deep, seeing all that you would show me.

Just a thought though, love…

…as I sit across from you, just looking again.

Yours in love and life,
Mpenzi wake

All the depths to you and I have yet to reach the bottom or find the most wonderful places.

Scholar

Monday, July 31, 2023
9:45 am

Mpendwa,

I made a promise to myself not to make these letters too poetic when I started writing them a month or two back. I just wanted to give my profound thoughts and all the love behind them. Because sometimes we all deserve plain talk and direct sentiments.

But what I want to say this morning for your last letter has a certain measure of poetry to it.

I found myself thinking back on our wedding. All at once memories flew back to the foreground like they had never left.

I remember standing in that tuxedo before God, our families, and our friends waiting for a new life to begin. Suffice it to say I was nervous, impatient, and happy all at once. The three took it in turns to overtake me as I stood there. There were some reassuring nods from people who I hold dear, and it steadied me, if I only for a moment.

A distraction came in the form of you and your father walking down the aisle. In my head I couldn't remember a better-looking dress or a more beautiful bride.

Off-the-shoulder, mermaid hem I remember you telling me. Even through the veil I could see you looking at me. I looked back, returning a tentative smile that I hoped offered comfort.

Your father and I exchanged a nod as he put your hands in mine. It's a trust I hope to live up to.

I couldn't tell you what the pastor said.

The vows? I remember those, though.

You said something that stuck with me. You said, "...today serves as the testimony of the good that God can place in your life when you allow Him to show you. My hope is to be the blessing of your mornings and the prayers before your goodnight..."

So far, you've been that and more.

I said, "...the curriculum of my life has become learning all that you will teach me about you. The lessons won't always be easy but nothing worth knowing is. And your worth cannot be measured. So, show me, instruct me. I will do the same for you. Today starts and I am anxious for the instruction."

And here we are still learning. It's something I hope to keep doing for as long as you'll let me.

I love you.

Yours in love and life,
Mpenzi wake

Teach me those things about you that you need me to know.

Afterword

It took great music to inspire great words. This is a list of songs in order that inspired each letter. A cool thing you can do is listen to each song as it pertains to each letter. I've done it myself and it was quite the experience.

Here's the list...

Come My Way - René & Angela

Constant Craving - k.d. lang

Grown Woman - Xavier Omär

Good Girls - Ye Ali

On You - Alon Crooks

Flowers - Wé Ani

Daydreaming - NxWorries, Anderson .Paak & Knxwledge

Glimpse Of Us - Joji

Stay True - Gāvhi

Picture You The Way I Do - Oleta Adams

ego talkin - Saint Harison

All That I Got (The Make Up Song) - Fergie feat. will.i.am

Conversation Pit - Junetober

Through The Night - Maeta feat. Free Nationals

No One In The World - Anita Baker

Noreg - Skye Townsend

Here - Kenyon Dixon & Susan Carol

Alone Together - Daley feat. Marsha Ambrosius

Better Than I Imagined - Robert Glasper feat. H.E.R. & Me'Shell Ndegéocello

I Don't Wanna Wake Up - Marie Dahlstrøm feat. James Vickery

Soul Shadows - The Crusaders feat. Bill Withers

phobia - DAMOYEE

I Want You - Marie Dahlstrøm and Elijah Fox

Rewrite Your Story - Song House & Kayley Bishop

Skin - Rihanna

Part II (On The Run) - JAY-Z feat. Beyoncé

Something To Say - Marie Dahlstrøm

Made For Me - Muni Long

Boohoo - Diddy feat. Jeremih

Good. Bad. Better. - Song House & Mikenley Brown

Calls - Robert Glasper feat. Jill Scott

Agape - Nicholas Britell

-LB

Acknowledgement

As with any acknowledgment, I want to first show my appreciation to the Most High for the talent and the words. These gifts You so freely offered are not for me but I love sharing them with the world around me.

I always have to thank my circle. You are the backbone to a lot of what I do. There is no stance that I can take that isn't possible because of you.

Finally...this is for you.

Yes, you. My future ever after. You've inspired me with the pictures of you yet to come and the memories waiting to be made with you. I'm thankful for that hope and you being the Muse that drives these words and all that I will ever be to you.

Thank you.

-LB